# Rising From The Ashes
## A Step-by-Step Guide To
## Chapter 11 Bankruptcy

# A Reorganization Primer
# for Entrepreneurs
# and Non-lawyers

## Includes Subchapter V and
## Important Sections of Chapter 11

### First Edition

# ARVIND MEHTA

**First Edition**
**Copyright © 2024**
**ISBN: 979-8-8839055-6-7**

# Disciaimer

"Rising From The Ashes: A Step-by-Step Guide To Chapter 11" provides general information and educational content related to Chapter 11 bankruptcy reorganization. A Chapter 11 bankruptcy reorganization guide serves as an introduction to understanding the principles, procedures, and implications thereof. Readers will gain a basic understanding of the Chapter 11 process through this book, which provides information about its purposes, eligibility requirements, benefits, drawbacks, and procedural steps.

Despite our best efforts to ensure that the information presented herein is accurate and complete, we do not intend for it to be taken as legal advice or as a substitute for professional advice.

Unless otherwise stated, this book is sold with the understanding that the author is not a legal professional, nor is he engaged in offering or rendering legal or financial advice or services. There is no attorney-client relationship established by reading this book, which is for informational purposes only.

Legal and regulatory issues relating to bankruptcy can be complex, subject to change, and may evolve over time. These laws and regulations can also vary depending on the jurisdiction.

It is important to note that this book contains no information specifically tailored for any individual or entity and may not be applicable in all circumstances. Readers should exercise caution and discretion when applying the concepts, strategies, and recommendations outlined in this book to their particular circumstances. To address specific questions or concerns related to their unique circumstances, readers are advised to consult with a qualified legal professional or financial advisor.

The author and publisher assert no liability for actions taken or omitted based on the information contained in this book. The content is open to interpretation and should be complemented by independent legal counsel. Reliance solely on the content herein is at the reader's own risk. Readers are urged to conduct thorough research and validate information prior to making decisions concerning Chapter 11 bankruptcy or any other legal issue.

By accessing and perusing this book, readers acknowledge and consent to the terms of this disclaimer, releasing the author and publisher from any and all claims, damages, or liabilities stemming from the utilization or interpretation of the information provided herein.

# Purpose of the Book

"Rising From The Ashes: A Step-by-Step Guide To Chapter 11" is an introductory primer for entrepreneurs and non-lawyers to help navigate the complex and unfamiliar terrain of corporate reorganization bankruptcy. In this essential guide, I have tried my best to demystify and explain the Chapter 11 process in the simplest and the shortest way possible, in an attempt to equip businesses facing financial turmoil with the information and knowledge needed to emerge stronger and more resilient.

Each chapter of this book offers a basic understanding of key aspects of Chapter 11 reorganization. From initial evaluation and decision-making to plan confirmation and emergence from bankruptcy, I have attempted to provide clear and actionable steps for every stage of the journey.

This primer will help you learn about the step-by-step process of Chapter 11 reorganization bankruptcy process so you can assess your company's financial health, develop a robust reorganization plan, and negotiate with creditors effectively. Discover the nuances of asset sales, debtor-in-possession financing, and the confirmation process. It will also help you gain insights into the role of various players involved, the importance of communication, and the legal frameworks governing Chapter 11 proceedings.

Whether you're a startup entrepreneur, business owner, a new executive in the C-suite, a board member or a non-legal professional, "Rising From The Ashes" equips you with the knowledge to navigate Chapter 11 bankruptcy with confidence and clarity.

If you read this book before your seek  legal advice and an expert guidance from a lawyer, this book is your indispensable companion and will provide you just the right amount of knowledge you need to ask your lawyer the right questions and hold a meaningful and productive discussion on your situation.

I dedicate this book to all the resilient entrepreneurs and business leaders who embarked on their ambitious, purposeful and adventurous journey of creating great businesses, took risks and faced financial challenges head-on. Please know, your courage, perseverance, and determination are of tremendous inspiration to others. May this introductory primer serve as a beacon of information and a source of practical guidance as you navigate the Chapter 11 reorganization process.

# Index

# 1

---

# INTRODUCTION

Discovering your company teetering on the edge of bankruptcy is an incredibly daunting scenario, fraught with anguish and uncertainty. The process of preparing for such dire circumstances can be equally formidable. Distressed by financial strain and grappling with cash flow constraints, organizations often find themselves compelled to swiftly pivot their business strategies in unanticipated directions. Actions that might appear drastic under normal circumstances suddenly become imperative in the face of adversity.

There exists a myriad of factors that can precipitate a company's descent into financial distress: flawed corporate strategies, ineffective management practices, sustained financial losses, inadequately competitive products or services, fierce competition, dwindling market share, and shifts in consumer preferences and market dynamics, to name a few. However, within the crucible of these challenges, lies the potential for revitalization through the implementation of restructuring and turnaround strategies.

Corporate restructuring and turnaround initiatives serve as retrenchment strategies aimed at rectifying past missteps, extricating the company from financial turmoil, and fostering its transformation into a robust and profitable entity once again.

While the terms "restructuring" and "turnaround" are often used interchangeably, it is crucial to discern their distinct nuances and implications.

Below explanation will give you a better understanding of Restructuring and Turnaround Management but I will keep the focus on Restructuring for the purpose of this book:

## Restructuring

Restructuring is a comprehensive overhaul of a company's operations, financial structure, or organizational framework. It aims to streamline inefficiencies, optimize resources, and adapt to changing market conditions through enhancing efficiency and reduce costs. It encompasses various measures, including operational streamlining, financial restructuring, and strategic realignment.

It is a strategic process undertaken by companies to realign their operations, finances, and structures to improve efficiency and adaptability. It involves reassessing business models, renegotiating contracts, divesting non-core assets, and implementing cost-saving measures.

Restructuring activities can be placed under different categories:

## Types of Restructuring

**Operational Restructuring:** Assessing and reorganizing business processes to improve efficiency and reduce costs. This could include outsourcing non-core functions, re-engineering workflows, or consolidating operations. This may include business process re-engineering, cost reduction initiatives.

**Financial Restructuring:** Addressing debt burdens, liquidity issues, or capital allocation problems. Financial restructuring may involve renegotiating debt terms, raising new capital, or divesting non-core assets to improve the company's financial health. Financial restructuring may include capital structure optimization, debt restructuring and Chapter 11 bankruptcy.

**Organizational Restructuring:** Adjusting the organizational structure, roles, and responsibilities to enhance agility, foster collaboration, and promote innovation within the company. Organizational change management, and cultural change initiatives.

**Strategic Restructuring:** Evaluating the company's business model, market positioning, and competitive landscape. Strategic restructuring may involve entering new markets, diversifying product offerings, or focusing on core strengths to enhance long-term viability. M&A, retrenchment, divestiture, spin-off, carve-outs, and product/service portfolio rationalization are some of the examples of strategic restructuring.

Restructuring may take place in various form:

## Expansion
- Mergers and Acquisitions
- Tender offers
- Asset acquisition
- Joint ventures

## Contraction

- Spin-offs
- Split-offs
- Divestitures
- Equity carve-outs
- Assets sale

## Corporate Control

- Anti-takeover defenses
- Share buyback
- Exchange offers
- Proxy contests

## Changes in Ownership Structures

- Leveraged buyout
- Going private
- Reorganization such as ESOPs or under IRC § 368

Since I just mentioned the reorganization, I would like to add that most private company acquisitions involve some kind of reorganization and may involve various types of proceeds such as cash, cash, and equity or just equity.

One important thing I intend to mention here is that an acquisition of a private company by another private company through an all-stock transaction typically falls under the purview of state corporate law rather than federal law. In an all-stock private company transaction, usually, there is no requirement for SEC filing unless some type of cash proceeds for securities are involved in the transaction.

For example, the California Corporations Code contains provisions related to mergers and acquisitions, and here are some relevant sections related to mergers and acquisitions in the California Corporations Code.

**Section 1100-1116** : These sections cover general provisions related to mergers, including definitions, requirements for approval by the board of directors and shareholders, and the procedure for filing articles of merger with the California Secretary of State.

**Section 1150-1159** : These sections specifically address the merger of domestic corporations with foreign corporations.

**Section 1200-1210** : These sections pertain to the merger of domestic corporations with other business entities, such as partnerships or limited liability companies.

**Section 1300-1313** : These sections cover the acquisition of a subsidiary's shares by the parent corporation.

**Section 1400-1415** : These sections outline the procedures and requirements for short-form mergers, which are mergers between a parent corporation and its subsidiary.

Such transactions may or may not have tax implications depending on various factors like state or federal taxes, stock basis and capital gains, asset basis step-up, employment and payroll taxes etc.

## Tax-free Reorganizations

Section §368 of the Internal Revenue Code (IRC) provides for various types of tax-free reorganizations, which allow companies to undergo certain types of mergers, acquisitions, or other restructuring transactions without triggering immediate tax consequences. These reorganizations typically involve exchanges of stock or assets between the acquiring and target companies, and they must meet specific criteria outlined in the tax code to qualify for tax-free treatment. Here are the main provisions for tax-free reorganizations under Section 368:

**Type A Reorganization (Statutory Merger or Consolidation):** A Type A reorganization involves the acquisition of substantially all of the target company's assets in exchange solely for voting stock of the acquiring corporation, and the target company then liquidates, with its shareholders receiving solely the voting stock of the acquiring corporation. Alternatively, a Type A reorganization can involve the merger of the target company into the acquiring corporation, with the target's shareholders receiving solely the voting stock of the acquiring corporation.

**Type B Reorganization (Stock-for-Stock Exchange):** A Type B reorganization involves the acquisition of the target company's stock in exchange solely for voting stock of the acquiring corporation. The target company may continue to operate as a separate subsidiary of the acquiring corporation.

**Type C Reorganization (Stock-for-Assets Exchange):** A Type C reorganization involves the acquisition of substantially all of the target company's assets in exchange solely for voting stock of the acquiring corporation. The target company then distributes the acquiring corporation's stock to its shareholders in complete liquidation.

**Type D Reorganization (Transfer of Assets to a Controlled Corporation):** A Type D reorganization involves the transfer of assets to a corporation controlled by the transferor corporation, in exchange for stock of the controlled corporation.

**Type E Reorganization (Transfer of Assets to a Controlled Corporation with Boot):** A Type E reorganization is similar to a Type D reorganization, but it allows for the transferor shareholders to receive "boot" (non-stock consideration such as cash) in addition to stock of the controlled corporation.

**Type F Reorganization (Change in Form or Place of Organization):** A Type F reorganization involves a change in the form of the acquiring corporation or a transfer of assets to a newly formed corporation in a different jurisdiction.

Reorganization is a form of restructuring and these are the main types of tax-free reorganizations outlined in IRC §368. Each type has specific requirements and conditions that must be met to qualify for tax-free treatment, and companies should carefully structure their transactions and seek professional tax advice to ensure compliance with the applicable provisions of the tax code.

## Turnaround Management:

Turnaround management focuses on reversing a company's decline and restoring it to profitability. It requires decisive leadership, careful analysis, and swift action. Key elements of a successful turnaround include diagnosing problems, developing a turnaround plan, implementing strategic initiatives, engaging stakeholders, and monitoring progress.

Key elements of a successful turnaround include:

**Diagnosis and Analysis:** Identifying the root causes of the company's problems through a comprehensive assessment of its operations, finances, and market position. This involves conducting thorough analyses of financial statements, market trends, and competitive dynamics.

**Developing a Turnaround Plan:** Formulating a clear and actionable plan to address the identified issues and restore the company's performance. This plan should include specific objectives, timelines, and performance metrics to measure progress.

**Implementing Strategic Initiatives:** Executing the turnaround plan with discipline and agility. This may involve implementing cost-cutting measures, restructuring debt, renegotiating contracts, or launching new marketing initiatives to stimulate demand.

**Stakeholder Engagement:** Engaging with key stakeholders such as employees, customers, suppliers, and investors to garner support for the turnaround efforts. Transparent communication and collaboration are essential to building trust and alignment.

**Monitoring and Adaptation:** Continuously monitoring the company's performance against the turnaround plan and making necessary adjustments along the way. Flexibility and responsiveness are critical as market conditions evolve.

## How Restructuring and Turnaround Help Distressed Companies:

**Addressing Root Causes:** Corporate restructuring and turnaround efforts delve deep into the underlying issues plaguing a distressed company, whether they stem from operational inefficiencies, financial challenges, or strategic misalignment.

**Restoring Financial Health:** Financial restructuring can alleviate debt burdens, improve liquidity, and optimize capital allocation, putting the company on a more stable financial footing.

**Enhancing Competitiveness:** Strategic realignment helps the company adapt to changing market dynamics, capitalize on core strengths, and seize new growth opportunities, enhancing its competitiveness in the long run.

**Preserving Stakeholder Value:** By taking proactive measures to address distress, companies can safeguard stakeholder interests, including those of employees, customers, suppliers, and investors.

**Unlocking Potential:** Restructuring and turnaround initiatives unlock untapped potential within the company, enabling it to emerge stronger, leaner, and more resilient in the face of future challenges.

A great restructuring and turnaround road-map encompasses reassessment of products, processes, people, suppliers, customers, operations, finances, infrastructure and organizational strategies, financial stabilization & internal control, and new capital infusion. It re-evaluates strategic options, redefining the strategy, developing plan for fundamental changes and financial restructuring, and focusing on value creation. The best restructuring and turnaround strategy is the one that is sustainable.

Turnaround management does not only apply to distressed companies, it in fact can help in any situation where direction, strategy or a general change of the ways of working needs to be implemented. Therefore turnaround management is closely related to change management, transformation management and post-merger-integration management. High growth situations, for example, is one typical scenario where turnaround experts also help.

An experienced restructuring and turnaround professional helps clients optimize the cost of capital and maximize shareholder value. This may involve changing the capital structure a firm has without changing the firm's assets i.e. either increasing leverage by issuing debt and repurchasing outstanding shares or decreasing leverage by issuing new shares and retiring outstanding debt by paying off the bondholders.

A good restructuring and turnaround strategy primarily focuses on stabilizing cash flow, restructuring outstanding debt obligations, reducing operating costs, reducing all non-essential costs, improving working capital management, improving product/price and product/market mix, streamlining product lines and accelerating the growth of high potential products & services.

Restructuring and turnaround not only require creative modification in the financial aspect of the company, it also take legal, regulatory, tax, ethical, social, and behavioral considerations into account. Without having an experienced restructuring adviser on board, restructuring can be real painful and complex process whereas having one ensures the achievement of company's financial goals.

# 2

---

# WHAT IS CHAPTER 11 BANKRUPTCY?

For businesses and other entities facing financial distress, Chapter 11 of the Title 11 United States Bankruptcy Code provides a legal framework that allows them to reorganize and become viable businesses in the future (*hence referred to as "Reorganization"*). Legal professionals, financial advisors, and entrepreneurs may need to navigate the complexities of Chapter 11 and therefore must be familiar with its nuances and intricacies.

Bankruptcy proceedings are supervised by and litigated in Bankruptcy Court, which is part of the Federal District Court system. Federal courts have exclusive jurisdiction over bankruptcy cases. They are not governed by the state laws.

Chapter 11 of the bankruptcy code offers businesses the opportunity to reorganize their debts and restructure their finances to avoid bankruptcy. Often referred to as "reorganization bankruptcy", Chapter 11 permits debtors to create a plan to repay their debts and continue operating. Under

Chapter 11 of the Bankruptcy Code, businesses may continue to operate while striving toward a successful recovery. This primer enables readers to gain an understanding of the key aspects and implications of Chapter 11.

When a company is facing financial difficulties but believes that if given time and a restructuring plan they can continue to operate, they may file Chapter 11 bankruptcy. A bankruptcy trustee is appointed by the court to oversee the bankruptcy process and ensure compliance with bankruptcy laws. The bankruptcy court allows companies to continue operating while under the supervision of a bankruptcy court.

The ability to restructure financial obligations is one of the key benefits of Chapter 11 bankruptcy. To avoid liquidation, the company needs to create a sustainable repayment plan that will allow it to continue operating and avoid liquidation. This can be accomplished by renegotiating debt, reducing or eliminating debt, or selling assets.

Chapter 11 bankruptcy also protects the company from creditors. During the bankruptcy process, creditors are prohibited from initiating or continuing legal actions to collect their debts. As a result of this reprieve, the company can focus on restructuring and developing plans to repay its creditors.

Chapter 11 bankruptcy is not a panacea for a company's financial distress. It requires substantial time and resources, and not every company is successful at resolving its financial challenges. A number of factors play a role, including the company's financial health, the severity of its debts, and the willingness of creditors to cooperate.

Companies that need breathing room so they can continue to operate and repay their debts may benefit from Chapter 11 corporate bankruptcy. This provides a legal path to reorganizing and restructuring their debts. Even though Chapter 11 bankruptcy is not a guarantee of success, it can be a valuable financial tool for distressed businesses requiring a financial turnaround.

# Different Approaches to Chapter 11 Restructuring

There are mainly two approaches to Chapter 11 restructuring-**Out-of-Court Bankruptcy** and **In-Court Bankruptcy** which may be a Prepackaged (also, Prepack) Bankruptcy, a Prearranged Bankruptcy or a Traditional Bankruptcy (also, Free-fall filing).

## Out-of-Court Bankruptcy

Out-of-court bankruptcy refers to a restructuring process that occurs entirely outside of formal bankruptcy proceedings, without court involvement and includes credit facility amendments, exchange offers, and consensual restructurings of liabilities. In an out-of-court bankruptcy, the debtor negotiates directly with its creditors to reach agreements on debt repayment, asset sales, and other restructuring measures.This approach allows for greater flexibility and confidentiality compared to formal bankruptcy proceedings but may require more time and effort to negotiate with multiple creditors individually.

## Prepackaged Bankruptcy (Prepack):

Prepackaged bankruptcy, often referred to as a "Prepack," is a structured bankruptcy process that involves negotiating and agreeing on a reorganization plan with key creditors before formally filing for bankruptcy. The reorganization plan is typically presented to the bankruptcy court along with the bankruptcy petition, and because key stakeholders have already agreed to the terms, the process can be expedited. Prepackaged bankruptcies are often used when the debtor has already secured support from a significant majority of creditors for the proposed plan, minimizing the need for extensive negotiations during the bankruptcy process.

## Prearranged Bankruptcy:

Prearranged bankruptcy is similar to a prepackaged bankruptcy in that key elements of the reorganization plan are negotiated with creditors before filing for bankruptcy. However, in a prearranged bankruptcy, the final terms of the reorganization plan are not necessarily agreed upon by all creditors before the bankruptcy filing.Instead, the debtor and a subset of creditors negotiate the main terms of the plan, with the understanding that other creditors will have the opportunity to vote on and potentially challenge the plan during the bankruptcy process.

## Traditional Bankruptcy (Free-fall filing)

Free-fall bankruptcy, also known as "free-fall filing" or "free-fall Chapter 11," refers to a situation where a financially distressed company files for Chapter 11 bankruptcy without having a pre-negotiated reorganization plan or the support of key creditors.

In a free-fall bankruptcy scenario:

**Lack of Pre-negotiated Plan:** Unlike prepackaged or prearranged bankruptcies, where the debtor has already negotiated terms of a reorganization plan with creditors before filing, free-fall bankruptcies are characterized by the absence of such pre-negotiated agreements.

**Limited or No Support from Creditors:** The debtor files for Chapter 11 bankruptcy without the support or agreement of its major creditors. This means that there is no consensus among creditors regarding how the debtor's debts should be restructured, assets liquidated, or operations reorganized.

**Uncertain Outcome:** Free-fall bankruptcies often result in a more unpredictable and contentious bankruptcy process. Without pre-negotiated agreements in place, the debtor may face resistance from creditors, competing restructuring proposals, and legal challenges to its actions during bankruptcy proceedings.

**Increased Risk of Liquidation:** Due to the lack of a pre-negotiated plan and creditor support, free-fall bankruptcies are associated with a higher risk of liquidation. Without a clear path to reorganization, the debtor may struggle to secure financing, retain key assets, or maintain business operations, leading to the possibility of asset sales and the dissolution of the company.

**Longer and Costlier Bankruptcy Proceedings:** Free-fall bankruptcies tend to result in longer and more expensive bankruptcy proceedings compared to prepackaged or prearranged bankruptcies. The lack of consensus among creditors can prolong negotiations, court hearings, and the development of a reorganization plan, increasing legal and administrative costs for all parties involved.

While out-of-court bankruptcy, prepackaged bankruptcy, and prearranged bankruptcy all involve negotiating restructuring terms with creditors before formal bankruptcy proceedings, prepackaged bankruptcies involve formal court filings with a pre-negotiated plan, while prearranged bankruptcies may involve fewer pre-negotiated terms and more creditor involvement during the bankruptcy process.

Free-fall bankruptcies represent a challenging and uncertain path for financially distressed companies, often characterized by heightened risks, contentious negotiations, and the potential for liquidation.

# 3

---

# RESTRUCTURING, TURNAROUND AND BANKRUPTCY: WHAT'S THE SEQUENCE?

The sequence of restructuring, turnaround, and bankruptcy for a company can vary depending on the specific circumstances and the goals of the stakeholders involved. However, there is a general framework that companies often follow when facing financial distress. Seeking professional advice from legal and financial experts is crucial in these situations. Here's a general sequence:

1.  Assessment and Analysis
    *   **Financial Assessment:** Evaluate the company's financial situation, including cash flow, liabilities, and assets.
    *   **Operational Assessment:** Identify operational inefficiencies and areas for improvement.

2. Restructuring:
   - **Operational Restructuring:** Implement changes to improve efficiency, cut costs, and enhance overall operations and profits.
   - **Financial Restructuring:** Renegotiate debt terms, seek additional financing, or restructure existing obligations.

3. Turnaround Management:
   - **Leadership Changes:** If necessary, consider changes in leadership to bring in experienced turnaround specialists.
   - **Strategic Changes:** Reevaluate the company's business model, product offerings, and target markets to identify opportunities for improvement.

4. Negotiations with Stakeholders:
   - Engage in negotiations with creditors, suppliers, and other stakeholders to reach agreements that support the company's recovery.
   - Consider debt-for-equity swaps or other financial arrangements to alleviate the burden of debt.

5. Out-of-Court Settlements:
   - Attempt to reach settlements with creditors and other stakeholders without resorting to formal legal proceedings.

6. Bankruptcy Consideration:
   - If out-of-court settlements are not feasible or successful, consider the possibility of filing for bankruptcy protection.
   - Explore the option of a Chapter 11 bankruptcy, which allows the company to continue operations while restructuring its debts.

7. **Chapter 11 Bankruptcy:**
   - If Chapter 11 is pursued, work with legal and financial advisors to develop a comprehensive restructuring plan.
   - Present the plan to creditors and the court for approval.

8. **Implementation of Restructuring Plan:**
   - Execute the approved restructuring plan, which may involve downsizing, selling assets, or making other strategic changes.

9. **Emergence from Bankruptcy:**
   - Upon successfully implementing the restructuring plan and gaining approval from creditors, emerge from bankruptcy as a restructured and more financially stable entity.

10. **Monitoring and Adaptation:**
    - Continuously monitor the company's financial health and performance.
    - Be prepared to adapt strategies as needed to ensure long-term sustainability.

It's important to note that this sequence may not be strictly linear, and some steps may overlap or require iteration based on the evolving circumstances. Additionally, the specific legal and regulatory frameworks may vary based on the jurisdiction in which the company operates. Consulting with legal and financial professionals throughout the process is essential to navigate the complexities involved in corporate restructuring, turnaround, and bankruptcy.

# 4

---

# PURPOSE OF CHAPTER 11 BANKRUPTCY

Using Chapter 11 bankruptcy, businesses may continue to operate while seeking relief from debts. This procedure provides a legal framework that enables them to establish a repayment plan that will enable them to survive and thrive as a reorganized business. The key objectives of Chapter 11 bankruptcy include:

## 1.     Reorganization

The Chapter 11 bankruptcy process enables companies to restructure their debts. This includes renegotiating payment terms with creditors and reducing their overall debt burden as a result of the restructuring process.

## 2.     Continuation of Operations

Unlike Chapter 7 bankruptcy, Chapter 11 bankruptcy permits debtors to continue operating their businesses with the guidance of a court-appointed bankruptcy trustee while still being in possession and control of its assets. Chapter 11 aims to preserve jobs, maintain relationships with customers and suppliers, and minimize disruptions to the economy.

In case of a public company, their stock continues trading during the court proceedings, however,  it gets delisted after failing to meet the listing requirements.

### 3.      Maximizing the Value of Debtor's Assets

Chapter 11 seeks to maximize the value of the debtor's assets for the benefit of creditors. By providing a structured process for the sale of assets or the reorganization of business operations, Chapter 11 aims to ensure that assets are used efficiently and that creditors receive the maximum possible recovery on their claims.

### 4.      Protection from Creditors

Chapter 11 bankruptcy provides debtors with temporary protection from creditors, preventing collection efforts and lawsuits.

### 5.      Fair Treatment of Creditors

Chapter 11 promotes fairness and equity in the treatment of creditors by providing a mechanism for the orderly distribution of assets and the negotiation of repayment terms. It allows creditors to participate in the bankruptcy process, vote on reorganization plans, and have their claims adjudicated by the court.

## 6. Financial Restructuring

The Chapter 11 bankruptcy process allows a debtor to restructure their debt in order to better address their underlying financial problems and to improve the viability and sustainability of their business. It facilitates the development and implementation of strategies for long-term growth and profitability following the bankruptcy.
For businesses that owe back taxes, the bankruptcy plan must include a mechanism to repay those debts. Unpaid taxes are not dischargeable in a bankruptcy. If such obligations are included in the bankruptcy plan, they must be paid back within five years.

## 7. Avoidance of Liquidation

Chapter 11 is often used as an alternative to Chapter 7 liquidation, which involves the sale of the debtor's assets and the distribution of proceeds to creditors. By providing a pathway for restructuring and reorganization, Chapter 11 aims to avoid the liquidation of viable businesses and preserve their going concern value.

Overall, the purpose of Chapter 11 reorganization bankruptcy is to facilitate the revitalization of financially distressed businesses, allowing them to emerge from bankruptcy stronger, more competitive, and better positioned for future success.

# 5

---

# ELIGIBILITY FOR CHAPTER 11 CORPORATE BANKRUPTCY

Under Chapter 11 bankruptcy businesses may restructure their debts and obligations. It is a complex legal process that allows corporations to remain operational while under the supervision of the bankruptcy court. It is imperative to understand the requirements for for Chapter 11 bankruptcy eligibility before filing.

This section provides an overview of the Chapter 11 process and the eligibility requirements for corporations.

## Types of Debts Covered

Both secured and unsecured debts can be discharged under Chapter 11. Businesses are allowed to maintain secured debts, which are secured against collateral, although the repayment terms may be modified. Chapter 11 also allows reorganizing unsecured debts that do not have collateral attached to them, but the priority of repayment may be modified.

## Requirements for Corporations

For corporations to be eligible for Chapter 11 bankruptcy, certain eligibility requirements must be met. As a business debtor, the corporation must engage in business or commercial activities and earn a regular source of income. It must also have debts exceeding certain limits. The debt limits vary according to the corporation's size.

The corporation must also comply with additional corporate filing requirements in addition to these requirements. Among these requirements are the preparation and filing of financial statements, a report outlining the proposed reorganization plan, and disclosure statements. As a result of these documents, the bankruptcy court will determine whether the corporation is capable of fulfilling its financial obligations and complying with bankruptcy laws.

During a period of transition, companies must attempt to improve their financial and operational performance, restructure their workforce, reduce costs, and find new sources for capital injection. Businesses that intend to restructure their debt must develop a realistic plan that indicates how they can reduce overhead expenses and continue operating their businesses. Using cost reductions or other support plans, the company provides creditors with a proposal detailing how the debt may be restructured. This proposal demonstrates to creditors how the business is capable of producing sufficient cash flow to maintain profitable operations while fulfilling its debt obligations.

Nonetheless, not every company is eligible to file for Chapter 11 bankruptcy. Chapter 11 bankruptcy is primarily intended for companies that have the possibility of reorganizing and continuing operations, rather than closing doors and liquidating assets. A company filing for bankruptcy reorganization under Chapter 11 must meet the following criteria:

**Type of Business:** The debtor can be a corporation, partnership, or an individual involved in business activities.

**Good Faith Requirement:** An insolvency proceeding must be pursued with the primary objective of reorganization.

**Financial Requirements:** The filing of a voluntary Chapter 11 bankruptcy petition does not require any specific financial or insolvency requirements. But in general, a company that is in a distressed situation, is highly leveraged, has very high Debt-to-Equity and/or Debt-to-EBITDA ratio, is in breach of covenants and is unable to pay creditors, will consider filing for Chapter 11 bankruptcy.

**Documents Required:** It is necessary for the debtor to submit a statement of financial affairs (SOFA) that includes balance sheet, a cash flow statement, a statement of operations, and federal tax returns with their bankruptcy petitions to the bankruptcy court. There are also additional documents required, such as a list of the 20 largest unsecured creditors who are not insiders, a disclosure of the compensation paid to the bankruptcy petition preparer, as well as a creditor matrix.

**Commercial Activity:** The debtor must engage in a commercial activity that is not a single-asset real estate business.

**Business Liabilities:** At least one-half of the debtor's liabilities must originate from business activity.

**Financial Distress:** Chapter 11 bankruptcy requires that a company demonstrate severe financial distress. This usually involves a decline in profitability, mounting debts that it is unable to repay, as well as an inability to meet ongoing financial obligations. A set of circumstances outside the control of the company must result in financial distress for the company, including economic downturns, changing market conditions, or unforeseen events

**Adequate Capitalization:** An organization must have sufficient capitalization or assets to reorganize its operations in order to be eligible for Chapter 11 bankruptcy. Chapter 11 bankruptcy will not be available to companies that have significant debt loads but limited or no assets, as the company's assets must exceed its liabilities, providing a cushion to repay their debts.

**Business Viability:** Chapter 11 bankruptcy requires a company to have a reasonable probability of success to qualify for the program. As part of the determination of whether a company can reorganize and continue to operate, the court will evaluate its business plan, market conditions, and profitability potential. In the absence of any viable business prospects, a company may not be eligible.

**Management Commitment:** Management commitment and active participation by executives are essential to the success of a Chapter 11 bankruptcy. It is important for the court to assess whether the company's management is capable and willing to implement the proposed restructuring plan. Ineffective or uncooperative management may not qualify for the program.

**Prior Bankruptcy Filings:** A company that has filed multiple bankruptcy cases within a specific period may not be eligible for Chapter 11 bankruptcy protection. Likely, the court will not grant Chapter 11 protection to companies demonstrating a pattern of habitual bankruptcy. The court may determine whether the company has a record of financial mismanagement or the likelihood of repeat filings.

**Compliance with Bankruptcy Laws:** All applicable laws and procedures must be followed by a company in order to qualify for Chapter 11 bankruptcy. Failure to comply with bankruptcy law requirements may prevent a company from being eligible for Chapter 11 bankruptcy. This includes filing all required documents, providing accurate information, and following court instructions.

**Subchapter V:** When filing for bankruptcy under Subchapter V, the debtor must specify that the bankruptcy is under Subchapter V, otherwise, the bankruptcy will be treated as a normal Chapter 11 bankruptcy.

**Role of a Trustee in Subchapter V:** As with standard Chapter 11 bankruptcies, the bankruptcy court will appoint a trustee to oversee a bankruptcy under Subchapter V.

As of 2023, however, eligibility for Chapter 11 Subchapter V bankruptcy filings by small businesses (please refer to the section "Subchapter V Bankruptcy") is generally limited to debtors engaged in commercial activity and with less than $7.5 million in secured and unsecured debts, of which at least half is derived from business activities.

**Tax Considerations:** Before or during the bankruptcy process, tax issues can present strategic considerations. Some of these factors may include preparing tax liability schedules, contesting Internal Revenue Service claims, expediting audits, filing IRS appeals, filing tax liens, and choosing a venue for litigation.

As long as the company meets the eligibility criteria outlined above, it can file for Chapter 11 bankruptcy and attempt to reorganize its operations and restructure its debts under a bankruptcy court's supervision. However, eligibility is just one factor, and ultimately the decision rests with the court.

# 6

# PLAYERS INVOLVED IN CHAPTER 11 PROCEEDINGS

Generally, a company in debt initiates the Chapter 11 bankruptcy process by filing the petition with the court. However, a creditor can also file an involuntary Chapter 11 bankruptcy petition against a company that is unable to pay their debt.

There are various players involved in Chapter 11 bankruptcy procedure:

### 1. Debtor-in-Possession (DIP)

A business that files for Chapter 11 bankruptcy protection remains in possession of their assets and continues to operate their business under the oversight of the bankruptcy court. A debtor-in-possession company is its own trustee in a Chapter 11 proceedings i.e. it manages its own assets and operations.

## 2. Creditors:

Creditors are the entities or individuals to whom the debtor owes money. Creditors may include suppliers, lenders, bondholders, employees, and other parties with financial claims against the debtor.

Generally, there are seven "classes" of creditors in Chapter 11:

- Secured creditors
- Priority claims (1. lawyer, bankers and trustee, 2. employee wages, 3. pension contributions up to 180 days prior, and 4. taxes)
- Sr. Subordinated claims
- General unsecured claims
- Subordinated unsecured claims
- Preferred equity interests
- Common equity interests

## 3. Bankruptcy Court

Bankruptcy court is the federal court that is responsible for overseeing the Chapter 11 bankruptcy process. The court reviews the debtor's reorganization plan, resolves disputes between parties, and eventually approves or rejects the proposed plan.

## 4. Bankruptcy Trustee

In some cases, the court may (or may not) appoint a bankruptcy trustee to oversee the administration of the bankruptcy estate and ensure compliance with bankruptcy laws. The trustee's duties may include investigating the debtor's affairs, managing assets, liquidation of assets and distribution of the creditors and mainly representing the interests of creditors.

Debtor-in-possession (DIP) and bankruptcy trustee are mutually exclusive for a single Chapter 11 filing i.e. a Chapter 11 proceeding may have either a DIP or bankruptcy trustee.

## 5. United States Trustee

The US Trustee is different than the bankruptcy trustee and is appointed by the Department of Justice. In a Chapter 11 bankruptcy case, a U.S. Trustee monitors the case and associated actions by all parties.

There are a total of 21 U.S. Trustee offices throughout the US, with a U.S. trustee appointed to oversee each office. Each U.S. Trustee employs staff, including attorneys to help in carrying out the Trustee's duties

## 6. Bankruptcy Examiner

The bankruptcy examiner is a person authorized to perform the investigatory functions of the trustee and is required to file a statement of any investigation conducted. If ordered to do so by the court, however, an examiner may carry out any other duties of a trustee that the court orders the debtor in possession not to perform.

## 7. Unsecured Creditors' Committee (UCC)

The UCC consists of the seven largest unsecured creditors of the company. This committee is appointed by the bankruptcy court to represent the interests of unsecured creditors (those without collateral). The committee may negotiate with the debtor, participate in the development of the reorganization plan, and advocate for the best possible outcome for creditors.

Unsecured creditors' committee:

- is appointed by the US Trustee
- consists of 7 largest unsecured creditors
- represents all the creditors
- helps shaping the reorganization plan
- investigates conduct of the debtor
- negotiates with the DIP lenders
- does not have power to "perfect a lien" i.e. can not make a lien legally enforceable

**Secured Creditors:** These are creditors who hold collateral or security interests in the debtor's assets. Secured creditors have priority over unsecured creditors in the distribution of assets during bankruptcy proceedings.

**Equity Holders:** Shareholders or owners of the debtor company who hold equity interests, such as common or preferred stock. In Chapter 11, equity holders may have limited or no influence on the restructuring process, as their claims are subordinate to those of creditors.

**Legal and Financial Advisors:** Attorneys, accountants, financial advisors, and other professionals who assist the debtor in navigating the Chapter 11 process. These advisors help prepare the reorganization plan, negotiate with creditors, and ensure compliance with legal requirements.

**Employees:** Current employees of the debtor company may be affected by the bankruptcy proceedings, particularly if there are layoffs, changes to employment contracts, or modifications to employee benefits as part of the restructuring plan.

**Government Agencies:** Depending on the nature of the debtor's business and the circumstances of the bankruptcy, various government agencies may have a stake in the proceedings. This could include tax authorities, regulatory agencies, or entities providing financial assistance or guarantees.

These are some of the primary players involved in Chapter 11 bankruptcy proceedings, each with their own interests and objectives as the debtor seeks to reorganize its finances and emerge from bankruptcy.

# 7

---

# IMPORTANT EVENTS AND TIMELINE

Normally, Chapter 11 bankruptcy cases last for anywhere between seventeen months to five years but in some cases, they can last even longer.

The following steps are relevant to a typical Chapter 11 business filing. Specifically, businesses that qualify as "small business debtors" under the bankruptcy code receive expedited treatment slightly different from regular Chapter 11 cases.

Even though a more detailed step-by-step process of Chapter 11 corporate bankruptcy will be discussed in the subsequent chapters, below is a quick summary of the process for a better understanding before learning about the timeline of important events:

## 1. Initiation of Bankruptcy Proceedings

Chapter 11 proceedings may be commenced voluntarily by the company or involuntarily by its creditors starting with the filling of a bankruptcy petition with an appropriate bankruptcy court.

## 2. Debtor in Possession Status

In a Chapter 11 proceeding, once it is initiated, a debtor takes over as "debtor in possession", thus maintaining operational authority over its commercial dealings and assets during restructuring. In certain extreme cases, however, where there are compelling reasons it may be necessary to appoint an independent trustee.

## 3. Automatic Stay

Upon filing the bankruptcy petition, there is a simultaneous initiation of an automatic stay that then prohibits creditors from taking any action against the debtor or its property until the resolution of the bankruptcy process. This prevents creditor actions after the bankruptcy filing. Automatic stay applies to all types of creditors, whether secured or unsecured.

## 4. Exercise of Avoidance Powers

The debtor in possession or his/her assigned trustee can avoid certain transactions such as transfers of money or property within a specified time before filing for bankruptcy through exercising avoidance powers. Such powers help protect the interests of all parties involved and ensure equal treatment of all creditors. Usually, this also takes in transfers done within 90 days before the case was filed and is employed to stop unfair preferential payments being made to particular creditors over others.

## 5. Disclosure Statement

As part of their duties, debtors must submit a detailed disclosure statement outlining their financial status to facilitate transparency among them during insolvency proceedings; this may include listing down who they owe money, itemized assets and liabilities plus a Statement Of Financial Affairs (SOFA).

## 6. Notice to Creditors and Filing of Proofs of Claim

All creditors named in the list are sent a notice of the filing as to the petition by the court clerk.Creditors and banks are informed that someone has filed for bankruptcy thus encouraging them to present their proofs of claim before a deadline.This process helps in settlement of creditor claims within bankruptcy processes.

## 7. Formation of Unsecured Creditors' Committee

The United States Bankruptcy Trustee establishes a committee that consists of unsecured creditors to represent the collective interests of unsecured creditors. This enhances transparency and oversight during restructuring process.

## 8. Formulation of Reorganization Plan

There is an exclusive period given to debtors during which they can submit reorganization plans detailing their plan for repaying debts and emerging from bankruptcy. Creditors will have the opportunity to vote on such plans afterward.

## 9. Court Approval of Disclosure Statement

Before voting on the plan, the bankruptcy court holds a hearing to assess the adequacy and sufficiency of the disclosure statement. 11 U.S.C.§1125(b) provides for a confirmation hearing at which time a judge will assess whether or not adequate information has been provided to creditors ensuring that creditors have sufficient information to make informed decisions.

## 10. Vote on Reorganization Plan and Confirmation Hearing

After approval of the disclosure statement, voting begins on the reorganization plan. Next, the bankruptcy and insolvency court holds an affirmation hearing to determine whether or not it meets three criteria: feasibility, good faith, and compliance with statutory requisites.

## 11. Plan Confirmation and Post-Confirmation Administration

Upon successful confirmation of the reorganization plan, the debtor is discharged from most pre-existing debts, thereby affording the debtor a fresh start financially. The debtor is subsequently required to adhere to the provisions of the confirmed plan and make requisite plan payments.

## 12. Final Decree and Case Closure

A final decree is entered, signifying the conclusion of the bankruptcy proceedings subsequent to the complete administration of the reorganization plan.

A status conference is held by the bankruptcy court within 60 days after the debtor files their petition with the court. A written report about the debtor's ongoing and planned efforts to develop a consensual bankruptcy plan must be submitted by the debtor 14 days before the status conference. The plan of reorganization must be submitted by the debtor within 90 days of the filing of their petition. The following table provides an overview of the timeline of various events:

| Timeline | Event |
|---|---|
| Filing a petition and case commencement | Chapter 11 petition is filed, automatic stay goes into effect and debtor continues to run business as debtor-in-possession (DIP) |
| Within first couple of days of filing petition | First day motion is filed |
| Within one week of filing petition | First day hearing |
| Within 14 days | List, schedules and statement of financial affairs (SOFA) |
| Within 20 days | Debtor presents proof of payment assurance to utility companies |

| | |
|---|---|
| 20-60 days | US Trustee convenes "341 meeting" with creditors and equity security holders |
| At the earliest opportunity after "341 meeting" | US trustee forms committee of unsecured creditors |
| Upon request of party in interest | US trustee forms committee of equity security holders |
| Upon request of party in interest | An examiner is appointed to examine debtors assets and liabilities |
| 60 days after filing | Status conference |
| 90 days after filing | Last day for debtor to remove pending state court litigation to bankruptcy court |
| 120 days after filing | Last day of debtor's exclusivity to propose reorganization/ liquidation plan |
| Within 90 days of creditor's meeting or 90 days after dividend notice | Deadline for government agencies to file proof of claim (general bar date). |
| 180 days after filing | Deadline for debtor to get approval for his reorganization plan unless court grants extension, creditors vote on plan, company's operations continue |
| Monthly reports | Monthly operating report is filed during the entire duration of the case until the case is closed |
| | Disclosure statement hearing |
| | Confirmation hearing (hearing on chapter 11 reorganization plan) |
| | Debtor fully/partially repays its debts (on pro-rata basis to creditors), court assigns an agent for 363 asset sales, restructure debt, modify loan terms, may offer stocks in lieu of debt repayment |
| | Final report |
| | Final decision and closing of case |

# 8

---

# IMPORTANT DEFINITIONS:

## Proof of Claim, Cramdown, Creditors Classes and Fulcrum Class

In cases where a creditor's name is absent from the debtor's submitted list or if there's a disagreement regarding the amount owed, the creditor is obligated to file a "Proof of Claim" with the court promptly.

For a reorganization plan to gain approval, it mandates the participation of all creditors in the voting process. Approval hinges on achieving a dual threshold: the plan must garner consent from creditors representing at least two-thirds of the total dollar value of claims and at least one-half of the total number of claims.

Should the voting fail to meet the aforementioned criteria, the reorganization plan proceeds to the next phase known as "Cramdown."

In a Cramdown provision a single **"impaired class of creditors"** (A class of creditors whose legal, equitable, or contractual rights are altered by a proposed Chapter 11 plan of reorganization, whether or not the change was adverse. For example, a creditor that is to be paid less than the full amount of its claim under the plan is impaired.) gets to vote ("affirmative vote") on the reorganization plan. These creditors MUST NOT include the insiders (officers and directors) of the company. This class of creditors is called the **"Fulcrum Class"** of creditors.

In the below table, Class 3 is an example of the Fulcrum Class:

| Class | Creditors & Equity holders | Recovery |
|-------|----------------------------|----------|
| Class 1 | Secured creditors | 100% |
| Class 2 | Senior subordinated claims | 100% |
| **Class 3** | **General unsecured claims** | **58%** |
| Class 4 | Subordinated unsecured claims | 18% |
| Class 5 | Preferred equity holders | 0% |
| Class 6 | Common equity holders | 0% |

# Non-dischargeable Debts

Businesses filing for bankruptcy are responsible for proposing a plan to repay some or all of their debts outside of excluded debts such as debts left off the bankruptcy petition, unless the creditor knew of the filing, unpaid taxes, fines owed to government agencies, debts arising out of tax-advantaged retirement plans.

A creditor may challenge your discharge if you file bankruptcy because it is not dischargeable from your bankruptcy.

Thereafter, the petitioner and creditors will have an opportunity to respond in case of a challenge by a creditor before debts are deemed not dischargeable. The court will then rule that the debt is discharged if no objections are raised by the creditor or if such arguments are deemed unnecessary.

A reorganization plan may include the sale of assets, reducing expenses, or obtaining new financing. These debts are generally repaid over several years, and some may be discharged completely.

# Section § 341(a) Meeting vs Status Conference

## Section § 341(a) Meeting

Many people get perplexed between section 341(a) meeting (also commonly referred to as 341 meeting) and status conference. The distinction here will clearly explain the difference:

Pursuant to the 11 U.S. Code §341(a), within a reasonable time after the **Order for Relief** (a court-issued order that initiates the bankruptcy process and granted in response to a bankruptcy petition filed by the debtor or their creditors) the US trustee shall convene and preside at a meeting of creditors. However, creditors are not required to attend the 341 meeting.

The United States trustee may also convene a meeting of any equity security holders.

341 meeting is generally convened between 20 and 60 days after the petition has been filed. In 341 meeting, the US Trustee and creditors can ask the debtor questions under oath about their

acts and conduct, address, schedules, assets, financials, properties (referred to as statement of financial affairs or SOFA) etc. It also aims to help the debtor to understand the bankruptcy proceedings.

### Status Conference

11 U.S. Code §1188 requires status conference in all Chapter 11 and Subchapter V cases. Under this section the bankruptcy court holds a status conference no later than 60 days after the entry of the order of relief.

Status conference can be postponed due to any circumstances for which the debtor can not justly be held accountable.

A debtor is required to file a "Status Report" with the court and also serve it to the US Trustee, creditors and other parties in interest detailing the debtor's efforts to attain a consensual plan of reorganization.

A court can also set a Status Conference on an adversary action or a contested matter. By understanding the issue between contesting parties and determining the time-frame needed, court can set issues for a continued hearing or later trial (also called **evidentiary hearing**).

# Section § 363 Asset Sale

Anytime a company files for Chapter 11 bankruptcy, the best way to make the repayment to the creditors is to either liquidate the assets or sell the entire company. If the debtor is able to demonstrate a **"substantial business justification"** for the sale of the business assets, the bankruptcy court will approve the sale of these assets under section 363 which allows the debtor to sell these assets **"free and clear"** of any claims.

*Section §3(a)(10) of Securities Act of 1934 grants exemptions to the securities issued in Chapter 11 of the US Bankruptcy Code. The section states: "The securities must be issued in exchange for securities, claims, or property interests; they cannot be offered for cash."*

*However, it is important to note that when options, warrants, or other convertible securities are issued in the Section §3(a)(10) transaction, Section §3(a)(10) does not exempt the later exercise or conversion. This is different than transaction exemptions under Section §1145 of the U.S. Bankruptcy Code. Section §1145 specifically exempts the later exercise or conversion from Securities Act registration.*

Section 363 asset sale is usually conducted in the following five steps:

1.    **Marketing of Assets:** An investment banker is often employed by the debtor to assist with the marketing of its assets. Many bankruptcy cases require the debtor to select a buyer who is the stalking horse bidder. This is the bidder that establishes the floor against which all other bidders will have to compete. A stalking horse bidder and the debtor prepare an asset purchase agreement, which is typically used as a baseline by other bidders.

2.    **Motion for Bid Procedure Approval:** The debtor submits a motion seeking approval for the stalking horse bid, setting the sale timeline, establishing bid submission requirements, and defining auction rules. These bid procedures, detailed within the motion, cover various aspects such as notifying involved parties, specifying the treatment of their contracts, setting deadlines for contesting proposed cure claims, and ensuring the purchaser's capability for future performance. Additionally, the bid procedures establish the time-frame during which objections can be raised against the sale of the debtor's assets to the purchaser.

3.    **Due Diligence and Bid Submissions:** The court notifies prospective bidders of the deadline for submitting their bids after the court approves the bid procedures. Based on factors like pre-petition marketing efforts and asset conditions, the time between the court's approval and the bid deadline varies. Section 363 sales are typically accompanied by limited representations and warranties, indemnity rights, or post-closing recourse for buyers. The debtor creates a data room for potential bidders. Therefore, prospective buyers should perform thorough due diligence on the company's assets and liabilities. The debtor should also inform contract and lease counterparties about conditions related to cure claims, objection deadlines, and the sale process.

4.    **Selection of Bid through Auction:** When the auction begins, the debtor announces the highest bid and describes the process in detail. After the auction, the debtor will announce the highest, or otherwise most favorable, bid. The auction procedure ensures an equitable price is achieved for the assets being auctioned. It is uncommon, however, for a lower cash offer to be selected as the winning bid in some circumstances. Several factors may affect this decision, including the certainty of closure, the expedited closing timeline, and the decision to maintain ongoing operations instead of liquidation.

5.    **Closing of the Sale:** Usually, the sale hearing is promptly scheduled within a few days after the auction. At this hearing, the Bankruptcy Court issues an order approving the sale of assets to the winning bidder. Bankruptcy courts often waive the 14-day stay required by bankruptcy rules for sales, allowing for expedited closure proceedings. These proceedings typically conclude within a day or shortly thereafter, following approval from the Bankruptcy Court.

# Stalking Horse Bid

A "stalking horse bid" refers to an initial bid on the assets of a distressed company that serves as a baseline against which other potential bidders can compete. The stalking horse bidder is typically selected by the debtor company through a competitive bidding process or negotiation prior to the formal auction of the assets.

Debtor convinces the stalking horse bidder to sign a non-exclusive, legally binding bid called Asset Purchase Agreement (APA) by offering various incentives. This asset purchase agreement requires the approval of the bankruptcy court and can not be executed without court's approval.

The benefits that a stalking horse receives may include:

1.      **First Mover Advantage:** A stalking horse bidder has the advantage of being the first bidder to set an initial bid price, which influences other potential bidders' perceptions of the assets' value and discourages low-ball offers. The first mover advantage of a stalking horse bidder also allows them to conduct extensive due diligence on the assets, giving them a deeper understanding of the potential risks and opportunities associated with the acquisition. This knowledge can give them a strategic edge in formulating a competitive bid.

2.      **Overbid Protection:** The stalking horse bidder is offered an overbid protection up to a certain amount i.e. other bidders can not overbid the stalking horse's bid by certain amount. It has to be more than the minimum overbid protection limit.

3.      **Break-up Fee:** If a stalking horse bidder is outbid and loses an auction, they receive a break-up fee as a form of compensation. This fee is meant to reimburse them for all of the

significant time, effort, and resources they put into the bidding process.

The break-up fee is to spur the stalking horse bidder on to submit a serious and competitive opening bid, letting them know that if someone else outbids them, then they still get compensated. It also works as a dissuasion to other potential bidders, as they might win the auction but have to pay the breakup fee.

Submission of a serious opening bid intrigues other high-quality initial bidders. It also establishes a floor price for the auction and speeds up the sale. A stalking horse bidder also gets more certainty, so they seriously commit to the auction process, which could maximize the value of the assets they're selling.

4.     **Favorable Terms:** In exchange for assuming the role of the stalking horse bidder, the bidder may negotiate favorable terms and conditions for the purchase, such as break-up fees, expense reimbursements, or asset protections, which provide some level of compensation and protection in the event they are outbid.

5.     **Due Diligence Reimbursement:** The stalking horse bidder either receives access to detailed due diligence materials and information about the assets, allowing them to conduct thorough assessments of the risks and opportunities associated with the acquisition or a reimbursement for the cost of due diligence they conduct on the asset being sold.

6.     **Opportunity for Competitive Advantage:** By participating as the stalking horse bidder, the bidder gains insight into competing offers during the auction process, enabling them to adjust their bid strategy accordingly and potentially outbid other competitors with a more informed and strategic approach.

7.     **Expedited Closing:** In some cases, the stalking horse bidder may be granted exclusivity or expedited closing timelines, providing certainty and efficiency in finalizing the transaction and reducing the risk of protracted negotiations or competitive bidding wars.

In general, serving as a stalking horse bidder can offer strategic advantages and financial incentives for parties interested in acquiring distressed assets while also providing the debtor company with a viable starting point for maximizing the value of its assets through a competitive auction process.

# 9

---

# CHAPTER 11

# STEP-BY-STEP PROCESS

As mentioned earlier, either a debtor can file a voluntary petition for Chapter 11 reorganization or creditors can file an involuntary petition asking the court to place the debtor in bankruptcy against its will. Any sale or financing of real property is subject to the approval of the Bankruptcy Court. Judgement and Liens remain attached to the assets until specifically released by an order to sell the assets "free and clear" (section 363 asset sale) of any interests, specific liens and judgement; or an order avoiding the specific    lien or judgement.

Section 303(a) of the Bankruptcy Code only permits involuntary cases under either chapter 7 or chapter 11 of the Code. No involuntary cases can not be commenced against a non-profit entity.

If the goal is only to liquidate debtor's assets, chapter 7 should be preferred but if the goal is the possible rehabilitation of the debtor, chapter 11 is a better choice.

The filing of an involuntary bankruptcy petition by a single creditor is usually not permitted. In order to file a petition, they must be owed a specific amount, which increases periodically and have fewer than 12 unsecured creditors on the debtor. In the event that there are more than 12 unsecured creditors, at least three must participate in the bankruptcy petition, and together they must meet a threshold amount of unsecured debt, which also increases periodically.

Below is the more detailed step-by-step Chapter 11 bankruptcy process:

# STEP 1: EVALUATION AND DECISION TO FILE

## A. Financial Distress Assessment

### Identifying Distress Signals:

1. **Financial Ratios and Metrics:** Evaluate financial ratios such as debt-to-equity, current ratio, and profitability metrics to gauge the company's financial health.
2. **Cash Flow Analysis:** Examine cash flow statements to identify liquidity challenges and cash burn rates.

3. **Creditors' Communication:** Monitor communication from creditors, especially if they express concerns or initiate collection actions.

### Exploring Alternatives:

1. **Debt Restructuring:** Engage in discussions with creditors to negotiate better terms, extended payment schedules, or debt restructuring agreements.
2. **Asset Sales:** Assess the feasibility of selling non-core assets to generate immediate cash and improve liquidity.
3. **Operational Efficiency:** Conduct a thorough review of operational processes to identify areas for cost reduction and efficiency improvements.

## B. Decision to File

### Board Resolution:

1. **Board Deliberations:** Conduct comprehensive discussions within the board of directors regarding the severity of financial distress and the viability of alternative solutions.
2. **Legal Counsel Engagement:** Consult with legal counsel to understand the legal implications and obligations associated with filing for Chapter 11 bankruptcy.

### Engaging Professionals:

1. **Legal Advisors:** Retain experienced bankruptcy attorneys to navigate the complexities of Chapter 11 proceedings and provide legal guidance.

2. **Financial Experts:** Hire financial advisors with expertise in bankruptcy and restructuring to assist in developing a comprehensive reorganization strategy.

## Business Viability Assessment:

1. **Feasibility Study:** Conduct a feasibility study to assess the likelihood of a successful reorganization and the business's ability to emerge from Chapter 11 as a going concern.
2. **Market Analysis:** Analyze market conditions, industry trends, and competitive factors to determine if the business model remains viable.

## Communication Plan:

1. **Stakeholder Communication:** Develop a communication plan for employees, customers, suppliers, and other stakeholders to ensure transparency and manage expectations.
2. **Employee Retention Strategy:** Implement strategies to retain key employees and maintain operational continuity during the bankruptcy process.

## Alternative Resolution Analysis:

1. **Liquidation vs. Reorganization:** Evaluate the pros and cons of liquidation versus reorganization, considering the impact on stakeholders, creditors, and the company's long-term prospects.
2. **Risk and Benefit Analysis:** Conduct a risk and benefit analysis of various courses of action, including the potential outcomes of bankruptcy proceedings.

Documentation and Compliance:

1. **Documenting Financial Position:** Compile detailed documentation of the company's financial position, outstanding liabilities, and assets to facilitate the bankruptcy filing process.
2. **Legal Compliance:** Ensure compliance with legal requirements for filing, including adherence to bankruptcy code regulations and any prerequisites outlined by the court.

The decision to file for Chapter 11 bankruptcy is a critical juncture that requires a thorough evaluation of financial distress, meticulous planning, and engagement with professionals who specialize in bankruptcy law and financial restructuring. The process involves a strategic assessment of alternatives, a clear understanding of the business's viability, and proactive communication with stakeholders to navigate the complexities of the bankruptcy journey effectively.

# STEP 2: PREPARARTION AND FILING

## Petition Filing

### Pre-Petition Planning:

1. **Reorganization Strategy:** Collaborate with legal and financial advisors to develop a comprehensive reorganization strategy. This involves outlining the key elements of the plan,

including debt restructuring, asset sales, and operational changes.

2. **Identification of Key Assets and Liabilities:** Assess the company's assets and liabilities to determine which are essential for ongoing operations and which may be considered for sale or liquidation.

## Filing the Petition:

1. **Submission to Bankruptcy Court:** Prepare and file the Chapter 11 bankruptcy petition with the appropriate federal bankruptcy court. The petition includes financial statements, schedules of assets and liabilities, a statement of affairs, and other required documents.

2. **Chapter 11 Voluntary Petition:** In a voluntary filing, the debtor initiates the bankruptcy process. Involuntary filings may occur if creditors collectively petition the court, but this is less common.

## Automatic Stay Activation:

1. **Immediate Protection:** Upon filing, an automatic stay goes into effect, preventing creditors from pursuing collection actions, lawsuits, or other efforts to recover debts. This provides the debtor with breathing room to formulate and execute a reorganization plan.

## Creditor Notification:

1. **Meeting of Creditors:** The court schedules a meeting of creditors, known as the 341 meeting, where the debtor must answer questions about

the financial situation and the proposed reorganization plan.
2. **Notice to Creditors:** Creditors are formally notified of the bankruptcy filing, including details about the automatic stay and the upcoming meeting.

## B. Automatic Stay

### Immediate Protection:

1. **Creditor Actions Halted:** The automatic stay immediately halts a broad range of creditor actions, including foreclosure proceedings, repossessions, and legal actions against the debtor.
2. **Breathing Room for Debtor:** The automatic stay provides the debtor with a temporary reprieve to assess its financial situation and negotiate with creditors without the immediate threat of legal action.

### Creditor Notification:

1. **Notice from the Court:** The court issues formal notices to creditors, informing them of the automatic stay and the commencement of the Chapter 11 bankruptcy proceedings.
2. **Prohibition on Communication:** Creditors are legally prohibited from communicating directly with the debtor about the debt during the automatic stay, funneling all communication through the bankruptcy process.

# STEP 3: INITIAL COURT PROCEEDINGS

The preparation and filing phase of Chapter 11 bankruptcy involve a meticulous process of planning, documentation, and court actions. This phase sets the stage for the subsequent reorganization efforts, providing the debtor with immediate protection through the automatic stay and initiating key court proceedings, including the formation of the creditors' committee and approval of essential motions such as DIP financing. The involvement of legal and financial professionals is crucial at every step to ensure compliance with bankruptcy laws and the development of a sound reorganization strategy.

## A. Formation of Creditors' Committee

### Committee Appointment:

1. **Court Decision:** Upon filing for Chapter 11, the court may appoint a committee of unsecured creditors to represent the diverse interests of various creditor classes.
2. **Composition & Representation:** The committee typically consists of the company's largest unsecured creditors and plays a vital role in negotiations and decision-making during the bankruptcy process.

### Collaborative Role:

1. **Negotiation and Mediation:** The creditors' committee actively engages in negotiations with the debtor to reach agreements on key aspects of the reorganization plan, such as debt repayment

terms, treatment of creditor claims, and potential asset sales.

2. **Representation:** The committee serves as a collective voice for unsecured creditors, ensuring their concerns and interests are considered during the reorganization process.

3. **Input on Plan Development:** The committee provides valuable input on the terms of the reorganization plan, creditor priorities, and potential asset sales.

## B. First-Day Motions

### Employee Retention:

1. **Key Employee Identification:** Identify key employees critical to the company's ongoing operations, reorganization and restructuring efforts.

2. **Motion Filing:** File motions seeking court approval to retain key employees and provide necessary incentives, such as retention bonuses or equity awards.

3. **Court Consideration:** The court assesses the necessity of retaining key personnel for the success of the reorganization and decides on the motion.

### Cash Access:

1. **Liquidity Requirements:** Evaluate immediate liquidity needs to cover essential expenses and fund ongoing operations during the early stages of bankruptcy.

2. **Motion Filing:** File motions seeking court approval for debtor-in-possession (DIP)

financing or access to cash collateral to meet short-term financial obligations.

3. **Court Approval:** The court reviews the motion, considering factors such as the urgency of the financing, its terms, and the potential benefits to the estate, before granting or denying approval.

## C. Debtor-in-Possession (DIP) Financing

### Negotiation:

1. **Lender Engagement:** Engage in negotiations with potential lenders to secure debtor-in-possession (DIP) financing terms including loan amount, interest rates, and repayment terms, which is crucial for funding ongoing operations and the restructuring process.
2. **Creditors' Committee Consultation:** Consult with the creditors' committee to address any concerns and obtain their input on the proposed financing terms.

### Court Scrutiny:

1. **DIP Financing Motion:** File a motion with the court seeking approval for the debtor-in-possession financing arrangement.
2. **Court Evaluation:** The court reviews and scrutinizes the motion, considering factors such as the necessity of the financing, its terms, and the potential benefits to the estate, before approving or denying the request.
3. **Approval or Denial:** The court issues a decision to either approve or deny the debtor-in-possession financing motion.

### White Knight and Stalking Horse Bid:

1. **White Knight:** In certain cases, a "white knight" may emerge—an external party willing to invest capital or acquire the business to facilitate the company's emergence from bankruptcy.
2. **Stalking Horse Bid:** Prior to a formal sale process, the debtor may solicit a "stalking horse" bid, setting a baseline offer for the sale of assets. This helps attract additional bidders and maximize value.

### Asset 363 Sale:

1. **Sale of Assets:** Under Section 363 of the Bankruptcy Code, the debtor may propose the sale of assets outside the ordinary course of business.
2. **Court Approval:** The court oversees the sale process, ensuring transparency, fairness, and maximum value for the estate.

The initial court proceedings in Chapter 11 bankruptcy are crucial for establishing the framework of the reorganization efforts. The formation of the creditors' committee, approval of first-day motions related to employee retention and cash access, negotiation and court approval of debtor-in-possession financing, and considerations of white knight scenarios and asset sales collectively set the stage for the more in-depth development and confirmation of the reorganization plan in the subsequent stages of the Chapter 11 process. Coordination and communication among stakeholders, including creditors, the debtor, and the court, are key elements in this phase of the bankruptcy proceedings.

# STEP 4: DEVELOPMENT OF REORGANIZATION PLAN

## A. Exclusive Filing Period

### Exclusivity Period:

1. **Court-Approved Timeline:** Upon filing for Chapter 11, the debtor is granted an exclusive period (usually 120 days, extendable to 18 months) during which only the debtor can propose a reorganization plan.
2. **Objective:** This period allows the debtor to assess its financial situation, negotiate with creditors, and develop a comprehensive plan for restructuring its operations and repaying debts.

## B. Disclosure Statement

### Drafting:

1. **Detailed Information:** Develop a disclosure statement that provides creditors with detailed information about the debtor's financial condition, the proposed reorganization plan, and the feasibility of the plan.
2. **Professional Assistance:** Work closely with legal and financial advisors to ensure the disclosure statement complies with legal requirements and effectively communicates the necessary information to creditors.

Court Approval:

1. **Submission to Court:** Submit the disclosure statement to the court for approval.
2. **Fairness and Adequacy:** The court reviews the disclosure statement to ensure it provides creditors with sufficient information to make informed decisions regarding the reorganization plan. If approved, the court allows the disclosure statement to be distributed to creditors.

## C. Creditor Voting

Plan Distribution:

1. **Creditors' Receipt:** Creditors receive copies of the reorganization plan and the court-approved disclosure statement.
2. **Explanation Meetings:** The debtor may conduct informational meetings to explain the terms of the plan to creditors and address any questions or concerns.

Voting Process:

1. **Creditor Classes:** Creditors are divided into classes based on the nature of their claims (secured, unsecured, etc.).
2. **Acceptance Thresholds:** The plan must be accepted by a certain percentage of creditors in each class for that class to be deemed to have accepted the plan.
3. **Cramdown:** In some cases, the court may approve a plan over the objection of certain classes if it meets specific legal criteria.

### Creditors' Committee Role:

1. **Recommendations:** The creditors' committee plays a role in evaluating the plan and may recommend acceptance or rejection to the broader creditor body.
2. **Negotiations:** The committee may negotiate with the debtor to improve the terms of the plan for the benefit of unsecured creditors.

## D. Confirmation of Plan

### Confirmation Hearing:

1. **Court Review:** The court holds a confirmation hearing to evaluate the feasibility and fairness of the reorganization plan.
2. **Creditor Objections:** Creditors or other parties may raise objections during the confirmation hearing, addressing concerns about the plan's terms and the treatment of their claims.

### Confirmation Order:

1. **Court Approval:** If the court is satisfied with the plan's feasibility and fairness, it issues a confirmation order.
2. **Plan Implementation:** With the confirmation order, the debtor can begin implementing the reorganization plan in accordance with its terms.

### Cramdown Provisions:

1. **Overcoming Objections:** The court may employ cramdown provisions to enforce the plan over the objections of dissenting creditors if certain statutory criteria are met.

2. **Fair and Equitable Treatment:** The plan must be deemed fair and equitable, ensuring that dissenting classes are not unfairly prejudiced.

# E. Emergence from Bankruptcy

## Plan Execution:

1. **Implementation Process:** Begin executing the reorganization plan, which may involve debt reduction, asset sales, operational changes, and other restructuring measures.
2. **Monitor Progress:** Regularly assess progress and make adjustments as needed to achieve the plan's objectives.

## Creditors' Payments:

1. **Payment Schedule:** Adhere to the payment schedule outlined in the reorganization plan.
2. **Creditor Distributions:** Distribute funds to creditors in accordance with the plan, prioritizing secured and unsecured creditors based on the plan's terms.

## Debtor Discharge:

1. **Successful Completion:** Once the plan is successfully implemented and all obligations are met, the court grants a discharge.
2. **Release from Liabilities:** The discharge releases the debtor from most pre-bankruptcy debts, marking the formal conclusion of the Chapter 11 bankruptcy process.

The development of the reorganization plan is a critical phase in Chapter 11 bankruptcy, requiring careful planning, negotiation, and court approval. The exclusive filing period allows the debtor to take the lead in proposing a plan, with the disclosure statement providing creditors with essential information. The creditor voting process and confirmation hearing involve significant court oversight, ensuring fairness and feasibility. Successful emergence from bankruptcy hinges on effective plan execution, adherence to payment schedules, and ultimately obtaining a discharge from liabilities. Coordination among the debtor, creditors, and the court remains crucial throughout this complex process.

# STEP 5: CONFIRMATION OF PLAN

## A. Confirmation Hearing

### Court Review:

1. **Purpose:** The confirmation hearing is a pivotal stage where the court evaluates the reorganization plan's feasibility, fairness, and compliance with legal requirements.
2. **Examination of Terms:** The court scrutinizes the terms of the plan, considering the treatment of different classes of creditors, the debtor's ability to adhere to the plan, and overall fairness.

### Creditor Objections:

1. **Opportunity to Object:** Creditors or other parties may raise objections during the confirmation hearing, addressing concerns related to their

claims, treatment under the plan, or the plan's overall viability.

2. **Court Adjudication:** The court adjudicates these objections, either approving the plan as proposed or requiring modifications to address valid concerns.

# B. Confirmation Order

## Court Approval:

1. **Positive Decision:** If the court is satisfied with the plan's fairness and feasibility, it issues a confirmation order officially approving the reorganization plan.
2. **Binding Effect:** The confirmation order makes the terms of the plan legally binding on the debtor and all creditors, establishing the roadmap for the post-bankruptcy phase.

## Implementation Commences:

1. **Immediate Action:** With the confirmation order, the debtor gains the legal authority to begin implementing the reorganization plan's provisions.
2. **Operational Changes:** The plan may involve significant operational changes, such as debt restructuring, asset sales, or renegotiation of contracts.

## Cramdown Provisions:

1. **Overcoming Objections:** If there were objections from certain creditor classes, the court may have

used cramdown provisions to enforce the plan over their dissent.

2. **Equitable Treatment:** Cramdown provisions ensure that dissenting classes receive fair and equitable treatment, even if they did not consent to the plan.

# C. Emergence from Bankruptcy

## Plan Execution:

1. **Implementation Process:** The debtor actively executes the reorganization plan, adhering to the terms outlined in the court-approved document.
2. **Ongoing Monitoring:** Regularly monitor the progress of plan implementation, addressing any challenges or unforeseen issues promptly.

## Creditors' Payments:

1. **Payment Schedule:** Follow the payment schedule specified in the reorganization plan, ensuring timely distributions to creditors.
2. **Prioritized Payments:** Priority is given to secured creditors, followed by unsecured creditors, as per the plan's stipulations.

## Debtor Discharge:

1. **Successful Completion:** Upon successful completion of the reorganization plan, the debtor achieves its primary goal of emerging from bankruptcy.
2. **Court Recognition:** The court officially grants a discharge, releasing the debtor from most pre-bankruptcy debts and liabilities.

## D. Post-Confirmation Adjustments

### Adaptive Measures:

1. **Flexibility:** The debtor may need to make adaptive changes to the reorganization plan if unforeseen circumstances or challenges arise during the implementation phase.
2. **Court Approval:** Significant modifications to the plan may require court approval to ensure fairness and compliance with legal standards.

### Continued Court Oversight:

1. **Ongoing Monitoring:** The court may continue to monitor the debtor's progress even after plan confirmation to ensure adherence to the agreed-upon terms.
2. **Stakeholder Communication:** Maintain transparent communication with stakeholders, including the creditors' committee, to address concerns and maintain cooperation.

### Potential Conversion or Dismissal:

1. **Monitoring Viability:** If the debtor encounters insurmountable challenges or fails to meet its obligations under the plan, the court may consider options such as conversion to a Chapter 7 liquidation or dismissal of the case.

The confirmation of the reorganization plan represents a crucial milestone in the Chapter 11 bankruptcy process. The court's approval provides the debtor with the legal authority to implement the plan, marking the beginning of the post-bankruptcy phase. Ongoing communication, flexibility in adapting to changing circumstances, and continued court oversight are essential elements for a successful emergence from bankruptcy. The ultimate goal is the debtor's successful reintegration into the business landscape with a strengthened financial position and a sustainable path forward.

# STEP 6: EMERGENCE FROM BANKRUPTCY

## A. Plan Execution

### Implementation Process:

1. **Timely Execution:** Following confirmation, the debtor actively executes the reorganization plan, adhering to the specified terms and conditions.
2. **Operational Changes:** Implement operational adjustments, debt restructuring, asset sales, and other measures outlined in the plan to achieve financial stability.

### Monitoring Progress:

1. **Ongoing Evaluation:** Regularly monitor the progress of plan implementation, assessing the effectiveness of the restructuring efforts.
2. **Adjustments as Needed:** Make adaptive changes if challenges arise, ensuring the plan remains on course for successful execution.

## B. Creditors' Payments

### Payment Schedule:

1. **Adherence to Schedule:** Follow the payment schedule outlined in the reorganization plan, allocating funds to creditors based on their priority and the agreed-upon distribution plan.
2. **Stakeholder Communication:** Maintain transparent communication with creditors, updating them on payment milestones and addressing any concerns promptly.

### Debtor-in-Possession (DIP) Financing Repayment:

1. **Repayment Obligations:** If debtor-in-possession financing was obtained, ensure timely repayment to the financing source as outlined in the plan.
2. **Financial Accountability:** Exercise financial discipline to meet all financial obligations and commitments specified in the plan.

## C. Debtor Discharge

### Successful Completion:

1. **Court Recognition:** Upon successful completion of the reorganization plan, the court formally grants a discharge.
2. **Release from Liabilities:** The discharge releases the debtor from most pre-bankruptcy debts and liabilities, signaling the completion of the Chapter 11 bankruptcy process.

### Post-Discharge Compliance:

1. **Adherence to Terms:** Continue to adhere to any post-discharge obligations specified in the plan, such as reporting requirements or ongoing financial commitments.
2. **Court Oversight:** The court may continue to exercise oversight during the post-discharge period to ensure compliance.

## D. Post-Confirmation Adjustments

### Adaptive Measures:

1. **Flexibility:** Acknowledge that unforeseen challenges may arise even after confirmation, requiring adaptive changes to the reorganization plan.
2. **Court Approval:** Significant modifications may need court approval to maintain fairness and compliance with legal standards.

### Stakeholder Communication:

1. **Transparent Dialogue:** Maintain transparent communication with stakeholders, including the creditors' committee and other interested parties.
2. **Addressing Concerns:** Promptly address any concerns or disputes that may arise, fostering a collaborative atmosphere for successful post-bankruptcy operations.

## E. Monitoring and Reporting

### Court Oversight:

1. **Continued Monitoring:** The court may continue to monitor the debtor's financial health and progress even after discharge.
2. **Compliance Verification:** Ensure ongoing compliance with the reorganization plan's terms and any court-imposed requirements.

### Financial Reporting:

1. **Regular Reporting:** Provide regular financial reports to the court, creditors, and other relevant parties to demonstrate ongoing financial stability and adherence to the plan.
2. **Transparency:** Transparency in reporting helps maintain trust and confidence among stakeholders.

## F. Potential Conversion or Dismissal

### Viability Assessment:

1. **Continuous Evaluation:** Continuously assess the viability of the reorganization plan and the debtor's financial health.
2. **Admittance of Challenges:** If insurmountable challenges arise, consider the possibility of converting the case to Chapter 7 liquidation or, in rare cases, dismissal.

## Court Decision:

1. **Court Intervention:** The court may intervene if the debtor encounters difficulties in maintaining the terms of the reorganization plan or complying with post-bankruptcy obligations.
2. **Consideration of Options:** Explore options with the court, which may include adjustments to the plan or other resolutions to address emerging issues.

The emergence from bankruptcy represents the successful conclusion of the Chapter 11 process. Vigilant plan execution, adherence to payment schedules, ongoing communication with stakeholders, and compliance with court-imposed obligations are paramount during this phase. The discharge from liabilities and the ability to operate without the constraints of bankruptcy signify the debtor's return to financial health and a fresh start in the business landscape. Continuous monitoring, transparency, and collaboration with stakeholders are essential to maintaining the gains achieved through the reorganization process and ensuring a sustainable future for the restructured business.

# 10

# BENEFITS AND DRAWBACKS OF CHAPTER 11 BANKRUPTCY

For businesses seeking to reorganize their debts, Chapter 11 bankruptcy has both advantages and disadvantages. As one advantage of Chapter 11, corporations are allowed to maintain control over their operations during the bankruptcy process, allowing them to continue their operations and adjust them as necessary. A Chapter 11 bankruptcy also provides a structured framework for debt restructuring, which allows businesses to negotiate more favorable repayment terms with creditors. We have already covered most of the benefits of Chapter 11 bankruptcy in the Chapter 4 of this book.

However, there are also significant drawbacks to Chapter 11 bankruptcy. The procedure is complex and time-consuming, requiring businesses to navigate a variety of legal and financial requirements. In addition to losing assets, Chapter 11 bankruptcy can result in liquidation if creditors can not satisfy their claims or is unable to successfully reorganize and get a repayment plan approved. It is also possible to lose customers as a consequence of the stigma associated with bankruptcy, which can negatively impact the business's reputation.

While Chapter 11 bankruptcy offers various benefits, it also comes with several drawbacks and challenges:

1.     **Costly and Time-Consuming Process:** Chapter 11 proceedings can be complex, lengthy, and expensive. Legal and administrative fees, as well as other restructuring costs, can quickly accumulate, draining resources from the debtor company.

2.     **Loss of Control:** While the debtor retains operational control of its business during Chapter 11, significant decisions often require court approval. This loss of autonomy can lead to delays and inefficiencies in decision-making processes.

3.     **Public Disclosure of Financial Information:** Chapter 11 requires extensive disclosure of financial information, which becomes part of the public record. This transparency may reveal sensitive or proprietary information that could damage the debtor's reputation or competitive position.

4.     **Creditors' Influence:** Creditors play a significant role in the Chapter 11 process, with the ability to challenge the debtor's proposed reorganization plan and negotiate terms that may not align with the debtor's interests.

5.     **Uncertain Outcome:** Despite the best efforts of the debtor and stakeholders, there is no guarantee of a successful reorganization or emergence from Chapter 11. If the plan is not

approved or fails to achieve its objectives, the debtor may face conversion to Chapter 7 liquidation or dismissal from bankruptcy protection.

6. **Employee Uncertainty:** Chapter 11 proceedings can create uncertainty and anxiety among employees about job security, benefits, and future prospects. Layoffs, wage reductions, or changes to employment terms may be necessary as part of the restructuring process.

7. **Market Perception and Stakeholder Confidence:** Public knowledge of a company's financial difficulties and involvement in Chapter 11 can erode investor confidence, damage customer relationships, and negatively impact the company's brand image and market value.

8. **Restrictions on Business Operations:** Chapter 11 imposes certain restrictions on the debtor's ability to conduct business, such as entering into new contracts or disposing of assets, without court approval. These limitations may impede the debtor's ability to pursue growth opportunities or respond quickly to market changes.

While Chapter 11 bankruptcy can provide a lifeline for struggling businesses, its drawbacks underscore the importance of careful consideration, strategic planning, and expert guidance to navigate the complexities and challenges of the process. For businesses and corporations, Chapter 11 bankruptcy provides an effective mechanism for reorganizing their debts and obligations. However, companies must understand the eligibility requirements for Chapter 11 bankruptcy as well as its advantages and disadvantages. By carefully evaluating these factors, businesses can make informed decisions regarding their financial future.

# 11

---

# SUBCHAPTER V OF CHAPTER 11 BANKRUPTCY

Subchapter V was added to Chapter 11 of the United States Bankruptcy Code in 2019 as part of the Small Business Reorganization Act (SBRA). This subchapter aims to streamline and expedite the bankruptcy process for small businesses, providing them with a more cost-effective and efficient path to reorganization. Subchapter V is designed to offer small businesses a chance for financial rehabilitation while maintaining ownership and control.

## Key Features of Subchapter V:

### 1. Eligibility Criteria:

**Debt Limit:** To qualify for Subchapter V, a business must have total debts not exceeding $7.5 million (as of the date of enactment, this limit was temporarily increased to $7.5 million from the original $2,725,625 under the Corona virus Aid, Relief, and Economic Security Act or CARES Act).

**Principal Activity:** The primary activity of the business must be commercial or business in nature, and it must be engaged in ongoing business operations.

## 2. Simplified Reorganization Process:

**Streamlined Plan Approval:** Subchapter V introduces a more straightforward and less formal plan confirmation process compared to traditional Chapter 11 cases.

**No Creditors' Committee:** In Subchapter V, there is typically no official committee of unsecured creditors appointed, reducing administrative complexities.

## 3. Debtor in Possession:

**Retained Control:** The business owner or debtor remains in possession and control of the business operations throughout the bankruptcy process.

**Trustee Appointment:** While a trustee is appointed, their role is more facilitative, and the debtor retains more control compared to traditional Chapter 11 cases.

## 4. Plan Confirmation:

**Debtor-Proposed Plan:** In Subchapter V, the debtor is generally allowed to propose a reorganization plan without the need for a competing plan from creditors.

**3 to 5 Year Payment Period:** The plan typically spans a period of three to five years, during which the business makes regular payments to creditors.

**No Absolute Priority Rule:** Unlike traditional Chapter 11, Subchapter V eliminates the absolute priority rule, allowing business owners to retain equity without paying creditors in full.

## 5. Creditor Voting:

**Majority Acceptance:** Subchapter V allows the court to confirm a plan even if one impaired class of creditors rejects it, as long as the plan does not discriminate unfairly and is fair and equitable.

## 6. Discharge:

**Broader Discharge:** Subchapter V provides a broader discharge of debts, including those incurred in the ordinary course of business after the bankruptcy filing.

**Debtor's Ongoing Earnings:** The discharge is tied to the debtor's commitment to use their future earnings for plan payments.

# Process Overview:

## 1. Filing and Eligibility Determination:

**Filing for Bankruptcy:** The small business voluntarily files for bankruptcy under Subchapter V.

**Eligibility Assessment:** The court reviews the eligibility criteria, including debt limits and the nature of the business, to determine if Subchapter V is appropriate.

## 2. Debtor in Possession:

**Retained Control:** The business owner continues to operate the business while the bankruptcy process is underway.

**Trustee Appointment:** A trustee is appointed to facilitate the reorganization process.

## 3. Plan Development:

**Debtor's Plan Proposal:** The debtor proposes a reorganization plan, outlining how it intends to repay creditors over the specified period.

**Creditor Interaction:** The debtor engages with creditors to negotiate and seek approval for the proposed plan.

## 4. Plan Confirmation:

**Court Review:** The court reviews and considers the proposed plan, ensuring it meets the criteria outlined in Subchapter V.

**Confirmation Hearing:** A confirmation hearing is held, where the court evaluates the plan's fairness and compliance with bankruptcy laws.

**Approval and Implementation:** If approved, the plan is confirmed, and the business begins implementing the proposed reorganization.

## 5. Post-Confirmation:

**Debtor Compliance:** The debtor adheres to the confirmed plan, making regular payments to creditors.

**Ongoing Oversight:** The court and trustee monitor the business's progress during the plan's execution.

**Discharge:** Upon successful completion of the plan, the debtor receives a discharge, releasing it from specified debts.

Subchapter V of Chapter 11 offers a tailored and more accessible bankruptcy process for small businesses facing financial challenges. It prioritizes the continuation of business operations, encourages negotiations with creditors, and provides a more efficient path to reorganization. Small businesses considering bankruptcy should carefully assess their eligibility and explore the benefits offered by Subchapter V in consultation with legal and financial professionals.

# 12

---

## CHAPTER 11 BANKRUPTCY:

## IMPORTANT SECTIONS

Title 11, US Bankruptcy Code covers total 9 chapters and 28 subchapters.

I am not going to cover all the chapters as the focus of this primer is only on Chapter 11 "Reorganization Bankruptcy".

There are two tables in the following pages -

- First table covering the overview of all the chapters, subchapters and sections under Title 11 Bankruptcy Code

- Second table covers all the important sections of Chapter 11 Reorganization Bankruptcy

# TABLE 1

| CHAPTER | NAME | SUBCHAPTER | SECTIONS |
|---|---|---|---|
| Chapter 1 | GENERAL PROVISIONS | | §§ 101 – 112 |
| Chapter 3 | CASE ADMINISTRATION | | |
| | Subchapter I | Commencement of Case | §§ 301 – 308 |
| | Subchapter II | Officers | §§ 321 – 333 |
| | Subchapter III | Administration | §§ 341 – 351 |
| | Subchapter IV | Administrative Powers | §§ 361 – 366 |
| Chapter 5 | CREDITORS, THE DEBTOR AND THE ESTATE | | |
| | Subchapter I | Creditors and Claims | §§ 501 – 511 |
| | Subchapter II | Debtor's Duties and Benefits | §§ 521 – 528 |
| | Subchapter III | The Estate | §§ 541 – 562 |
| Chapter 7 | LIQUIDATION | | |
| | Subchapter I | Officers and Administration | §§ 701 – 707 |
| | Subchapter II | Collection, Liquidation and Distribution of the Estate | §§ 721 – 727 |
| | Subchapter III | Stockbroker Liquidation | §§ 741 – 753 |
| | Subchapter IV | Commodity Broker Liquidation | §§ 761 – 767 |
| | Subchapter V | Clearing Bank Liquidation | §§ 781 – 784 |

| Chapter 9 | ADJUSTMENT OF DEBTS OF A MUNICIPALITY | | |
|---|---|---|---|
| | Subchapter I | General Provision | §§ 901 – 904 |
| | Subchapter II | Administration | §§ 921 – 930 |
| | Subchapter III | The Plan | §§ 941 – 946 |
| Chapter 11 | REORGANIZATION | | |
| | Subchapter I | Officers and Administration | §§ 1101 – 1116 |
| | Subchapter II | The Plan | §§ 1121 – 1129 |
| | Subchapter III | Post Confirmation Matters | §§ 1141 – 1146 |
| | Subchapter IV | Railroad Reorganization | §§ 1161 – 1174 |
| | Subchapter V | Small Business Debtor Reorganization | §§ 1181 – 1195 |
| Chapter 12 | ADJUSTMENTS OF DEBT OF A FAMILY FARMER OR A FISHERMAN WITH A REGULAR ANNUAL INCOME | | |
| | Subchapter I | Officers, Administration and The Estate | §§ 1201 – 1208 |
| | Subchapter II | The Plan | §§ 1221 – 1231 |
| Chapter 13 | ADJUSTMENT OF DEBTS OF AN INDIVIDUAL WITH REGULAR INCOME | | |
| | Subchapter I | Officers, Administration and The Estate | §§ 1301 – 1308 |
| | Subchapter II | The Plan | §§ 1321 – 1330 |

| Chapter 15 | **ANCILLIARY AND OTHER CROSS-BORDER CASES** | | |
|---|---|---|---|
| | Subchapter I | Gen. Provisions | §§ 1501 – 1508 |
| | Subchapter II | Access of Foreign Representatives and Creditors to the Court | §§ 1509 – 1514 |
| | Subchapter III | Recognition of a Foreign Proceeding and Relief | §§ 1515 – 1524 |
| | Subchapter IV | Cooperation with Foreign Courts and Foreign Representatives | §§ 1525 – 1527 |
| | Subchapter V | Concurrent Proceedings | §§ 1528 – 1532 |

# TABLE 2

| CHAPTER 11: REORGANIZATION | DESCRIPTION |
|---|---|
| Section § 105 | Defines the power of court |
| Section § 107 | Defines that a paper filed in a case under Title 11 and the dockets of a bankruptcy court are public records and open to examination by an entity at reasonable times without charge |
| Section § 108 | Defines the provisions for the extension of time |
| Section § 112 | Prohibits the disclosure of name of minor children |
| Section § 303 | Outlines the circumstances under which creditors can file an **involuntary bankruptcy petition** against a debtor, potentially leading to a Chapter 11 case. |
| Section § 305 | After notice and hearing, a court may dismiss a case under this title or may suspend all proceedings at any time if the interest of debtor and creditors can be better served by such dismissal |
| Section § 307 | The United States Trustee may raise, appear and be heard on any issue in any case under this title but may not file a plan pursuant to section § 1121 |
| Section § 308 | Describes the **debtor's reporting requirements** |
| Section § 321 | Defines eligibility to serve as trustee |
| Section § 322 | Defines qualification of trustee |
| Section § 323 | Defines role and capacity of trustee |
| Section § 324 | Defines court may remove a trustee, other than United States trustee, or an examiner for cause |

| Section § 326 | Limitation on compensation of trustee |
|---|---|
| Section § 341 | Defines within a reasonable time after the order for relief, the United States trustee may convene and preside at a **meeting of creditors** or any equity security holders |
| Section § 343 | Defines the debtor shall appear and submit to examination under oath at "341 meeting" and may be examined by any creditors, trustee or the United State trustee. |
| Section § 362 | Defines the provisions for and grants **Automatic Stay** |
| Section § 363(d) | Allows parties, under specific circumstances, to seek **relief from the automatic stay** imposed by Section 362, enabling them to proceed with certain actions against the debtor. |
| Section § 363 | Defines the provision for Use, Sales or Lease of Property in a case filed under this title |
| Section § 364 | Defines that if a trustee is authorized to operate the business of the debtor, trustee may obtain unsecured debt in the ordinary course of business |
| Section § 365 | Debtors can assume or reject Executory contracts and unexpired leases, allowing them to retain beneficial contracts or rid themselves of burdensome ones. The court must approve such assumptions or rejections, ensuring fairness to both the debtor and the affected parties. |
| Section § 366 | A utility company may not alter, refuse or discontinue service to trustee or debtor solely on the basis of commencement of a case under this title |

| | |
|---|---|
| Section § 501 | Defines the filing a proof of claim by creditor and filing a proof of interest by a security holder |
| Section § 503 | Defines allowance of administrative expenses |
| Section § 505 | Define the determination of tax liability |
| Section § 506 | Outlines the treatment of secured claims in bankruptcy, including the determination of the value of collateral and the rights of secured creditors. |
| Section § 507 | Determines the priority of expenses and claims |
| Section § 521 | Defines duties of debtor |
| Section § 522 | Defines the exemptions from claims allowed to debtor and also permits a person to voluntarily waive a right to claim exemptions |
| Section § 541 | Defines what constitutes the bankruptcy estate, encompassing all legal or equitable interests of the debtor in property as of the commencement of the case. Also, specifies inclusions and exclusions, helping determine which assets are available for distribution among creditors. |
| Section § 547 | This section allows the bankruptcy trustee or debtor in possession to **avoid certain preferential transfers** made by the debtor to creditors within a specified period before the bankruptcy filing. |
| Section § 548 | Empowers the bankruptcy trustee or debtor in possession to **avoid fraudulent transfers** made by the debtor with the intent to defraud, hinder, or delay creditors. |

| | |
|---|---|
| Section § 1102 | Defines the formation and role of creditors' and equity committees in representing the interests of different creditor classes during bankruptcy proceedings. **(Creditors' and Equity Committees)** |
| Section § 1106 | Outlines the **duties and powers of the debtor in possession and Examiner** (by court order), emphasizing the fiduciary responsibility to manage the business in the best interests of creditors. |
| Section § 1107 | This section designates the debtor as the **"debtor in possession,"** allowing the company's existing management to continue operating the business during the bankruptcy process. The debtor in possession has the authority to manage the business, initiate lawsuits, and perform other duties, subject to court oversight. |
| Section § 1113 | Provides a framework for the debtor to seek court approval to modify or reject existing **collective bargaining agreements** with unions. |
| Section § 1122 | Outlines the criteria for the **classification of claims** and interests in a reorganization plan, facilitating the fair and equitable treatment of creditors. |
| Section § 1123 | Specifies the required elements of a reorganization plan **("content of the plan")**, including the treatment of various classes of claims and interests. Outlines the criteria for classifying claims and interests and the treatment each class will receive under the plan. |

| | |
|---|---|
| Section § 1125 | This section outlines the requirements for the disclosure statement accompanying the reorganization plan **(Post-petition disclosure and solicitation)** . It must provide adequate information for creditors to make an informed decision on the plan. The court must approve the disclosure statement before it is distributed to creditors. **(Court approval of disclosure statement)** |
| Section § 1126 | Describes the requirements for the acceptance of a reorganization plan by creditors and equity security holders, including the necessary voting majorities. **(Acceptance or rejection of plan)** |
| Section § 1127 | Allows for the **modification of a confirmed plan** under certain circumstances, providing flexibility if unforeseen challenges arise. |
| Section § 1128 | Discusses that after notice, the court shall hold a **hearing on confirmation** of a plan and a party in interest may object to confirmation of a plan. |
| Section § 1129 | Outlines the criteria that a reorganization plan must satisfy for court approval, including the fair and equitable treatment of creditors and feasibility of the plan. **(Confirmation of plan)** |
| Section § 1129(a)(10) | Discuss the **acceptance of plan by impaired classes** and specifies that at least one impaired class of creditors must accept the plan for it to be eligible for confirmation. |
| Section § 1129(a)(11) | Ensures that administrative expenses are provided for in the reorganization plan, facilitating the smooth |

| | |
|---|---|
| | administration of the bankruptcy case. |
| Section § 1129(b) | Provides the court with the authority to confirm a plan even if not all classes of creditors accept it, under specific circumstances, such as when the plan is fair and equitable. **(Cramdown provision)** |
| Section § 1129(a)(15) | Requires that each class of creditors must receive at least as much under the plan as it would in a Chapter 7 liquidation. **(Best Interests of Creditors Test)** |
| Section § 1141 | Upon confirmation of the reorganization plan, it becomes binding on the debtor, creditors, and other parties involved. **(Binding effect of plan confirmation)** |
| Section § 1141(d) | Details the conditions under which a debtor is granted a discharge from most pre-bankruptcy debts upon the successful completion of the reorganization plan. **(Debtor's discharge)** |
| Section § 1142 | Addresses the **implementation of the reorganization plan**, specifying the steps and processes required to carry out the plan's provisions. |
| Section § 1143 | Defines that if a plan requires presentment or surrender of a security or the performance of any other act as a condition to participation in distribution under the plan, such action shall be taken not later than five years after the date of the entry of the order of confirmation. Any entity that has not within such time presented or surrendered such entity's security or taken any such other action that the |

| | |
|---|---|
| | plan requires may not participate in distribution under the plan. |
| Section § 1144 | Under this section, on request of a party in interest at any time before 180 days after the date of the entry of the order of confirmation, and after notice and a hearing, the court may revoke such order if and only if such order was procured by fraud. |
| Section § 1145 Shares or 1145 Rights Offering | 1145 Rights Offering means the rights offering for shares of New Common Stock to be conducted in reliance upon the exemption from registration under the Securities Act provided in section 1145 of the Bankruptcy Code, in accordance with the 1145 Rights Offering Procedures. Section 1145 is an exemption from the registration requirements of Section 5 of the Securities Act of 1933, under which it is unlawful to offer or sell any security unless a registration statement is in effect with respect to the security, or an exemption from registration is available. It also provides an exemption from the registration requirements of state securities laws. A key consideration for investors in securities of bankrupt issuers is the extent to which the securities received upon consummation of a Chapter 11 plan will be freely transferable. |

| | |
|---|---|
| **Section § 1145(a)** | Among other things, Section 1145(a) exempts from registration offers or sales under a plan of reorganization of securities principally in exchange for a claim against, or an interest in, a debtor or its affiliate. |
| **Section § 1145(a)(3)** | Section 1145(a)(3) grants a debtor in possession or trustee in chapter 11 an extremely narrow portfolio **security exemption from section 5 of the Securities Act of 1933** [15 U.S.C. 77e] or any comparable State law. Section 1145(a)(3) also permits the trustee to distribute 4 percent of the securities during the 2-year period immediately following the date of the filing of the petition. In addition, the security must be of a reporting company under section 13 of the Securities and Exchange Act of 1934 [15 U.S.C. 78m], and must be in compliance with all applicable requirements for the continuing of trading in the security on the date that the trustee offers or sells the security. |
| **Section § 1146** | Discusses that the issuance, transfer, or exchange of a security, or the making or delivery of an instrument of transfer under a plan confirmed under section 1129 or 1191 of this title, may not be taxed under any law imposing a stamp tax or similar tax. **(Special tax provisions)** |
| **Section § 1188** | Mandates status conference |
| **Section § 1191** | Defines and describes the Subchapter V - SMALL BUSINESS DEBTOR REORGANIZATION plan confirmation |

# 13

---

## Epilogue

As soon as the Chapter 11 bankruptcy process completes and all stakeholders can participate in the company's reorganization process, a significant milestone is reached. Because of the challenging phase of financial distress, a crucial opportunity for strategic renewal and revitalization emerges.

With the assistance of the debtor, creditors, legal advisors, and bankruptcy court oversight, bankruptcy court reorganization plans are meticulously crafted, refined, and ultimately confirmed. In addition to addressing financial challenges, restructuring obligations, the plan outlines a path to sustainable growth.

Following the approval of a reorganization plan, a debtor emerges from bankruptcy with renewed purpose and strengthened financial resources. As part of the discharge of debts, operational changes and debt restructuring are implemented, providing the company with a fresh start and a brighter future as part of the discharge of debts.

A confirmation of the plan means a resolution of creditors' claims and a way to recover for them. Although concessions may have been made, the reorganization plan ensures fair treatment and maximizes the company's value for distribution.

Transparency, communication, and cooperation are of utmost importance throughout the Chapter 11 reorganization bankruptcy process. All the creditors, stakeholders and other parties in interest navigate complex legal frameworks, negotiate in good faith, and work towards a common objective of preserving value and ensuring the company's long-term viability.

The company emerges from bankruptcy with a renewed sense of resilience and determination. Lessons learned from the restructuring process serve as valuable insights, guiding future decision-making and fostering a culture of financial prudence and risk management.

While the Chapter 11 journey is strenuous, it is also tremendously transformative. It provides an opportunity for introspection, retrospection, need for a change in organizational culture, technological innovations, and strategic realignment, positioning the company for success in an ever-evolving global business landscape.

With the last strike of the gavel, the Chapter 11 proceedings draw to a close. Yet, this closure paves the way for a fresh start, a new phase characterized by tenacity, expansion, and an unshakable commitment to transformation. The company now stands more robust, more flexible, and primed to seize the forthcoming opportunities.

This signals the end of the Chapter 11 proceedings, it also marks the beginning of a new chapter, a chapter defined by resilience, growth, and the unwavering spirit of reinvention. The company emerges stronger, more adaptive, and ready to embrace a new and brighter future.

# About the Author

Arvind Mehta stands at the intersection of technology entrepreneurship, strategic advisory, and financial acumen, bringing multifaceted expertise to the corporate world. His industry experience spans over two decades encompassing corporate finance, mergers & acquisitions, capital markets, and corporate governance, showcasing his deep understanding of the corporate landscape.

With over 20 years in the corporate realm, he has earned recognition for his versatile expertise across various domains. Acknowledged as a polymath among his peers, Arvind has undertaken multifaceted roles in corporate advisory, management consulting, supply chain, and digital transformation.

Currently serving as the Managing Partner at Ducat Capital Partners, Arvind oversees private equity investments in the Manufacturing, Logistics & Distribution B2B sectors. Concurrently, he holds the positions of Founder, President & CEO at Touchstone ITS, a management consulting and digital transformation services firm that helps high-revenue companies with supply chain and asset intensive operations. Arvind has been a catalyst for innovation, driving organizational excellence in some of the largest companies in the United States.

His previous leadership roles in investment banking and corporate finance further enhanced his expertise, highlighting his strategic acumen and dedication to corporate excellence.

Arvind serves as the corporate board advisor at EPSoft Inc, a technology consulting firm that leverages the combination of process mining and business intelligence for robotic process automation through it's AI powered intelligent automation platform.

Beyond the boardroom, Arvind's impact extends to the vibrant startup landscape. His role as a board member on the boards of "Rush49", an online marketplace for outdoor recreational activities and "REMO Homes", an innovative manufacturing company that founded by former SpaceX executives and NASA scientists that manufactures smart modular homes has not only exposed him to the cutting edge of technology but has also deepened his understanding of corporate governance in dynamic, and high-growth environments.

This book is a synthesis of his rich and varied experiences. It aims to simplify the intricate process of Chapter 11 bankruptcy. Through his book, Arvind extends an invitation to entrepreneurs, non-legal professionals and autodidacts who aspire to learn Chapter 11 bankruptcy fundamentals and explore it through his strategic insights garnered from his extensive journey at the forefront of business leadership.

www.ingramcontent.com/pod-product-compliance
Lightning Source LLC
Chambersburg PA
CBHW071052290526
45795CB00004B/1451